Massimo Wolke

Animals with Cocks

Coloring Book

Massimo Wolke

Animals with Cocks

Coloring Book

Bibliografische Information der Deutschen Nationalbibliothek:
Die Deutsche Nationalbibliothek verzeichnet diese Publikation in der
Deutschen Nationalbibliografie; detaillierte bibliografische Daten sind im
Internet über http://dnb.dnb.de abrufbar.

© 2017 Massimo Wolke
Herstellung und Verlag:
BoD – Books on Demand, Norderstedt

ISBN: 978-3-7448-9340-4